EMPANADAS

Clarkson N. Potter, Inc./Publishers NEW YORK
DISTRIBUTED BY CROWN PUBLISHERS, INC.

EMPANADAS
& Other International Turnovers

60 Easy Low-Salt, Low-Fat Recipes

George & Sherry LaFollette Zabriskie

Published by Clarkson N. Potter, Inc.,
One Park Avenue, New York, New York 10016 and simultaneously in Canada by General Publishing Company Limited

Manufactured in the United States of America

"Argentine Spiced Beef Empanada," page 54, reprinted by permission of *Woman's Day* magazine. Copyright © 1980 by CBS Publications, the Consumer Publishing Division of CBS Inc.

"Chicken Paprikash Empanada," page 63, and "Ricotta Surprise," page 90, reprinted by permission of the *New York Post*.

LIBRARY OF CONGRESS CATALOGING IN PUBLICATION DATA

Zabriskie, Sherry.
Empanadas.

Includes index.
1. Turnovers (Cookery)   2. Cookery, International.
I. Zabriskie, George Albert, 1926–   .   II. Title.
TX770.Z3   1983   641.8   82-16173
ISBN: 0-517-547562

Designed by Gael Towey Dillon

Illustrations by Andrzej Czeczot

10 9 8 7 6 5 4 3 2 1

First Edition

CONTENTS

▲▲▲▲▲▲▲▲▲▲▲▲▲▲▲▲▲▲

We dedicate this book with lasting affection and appreciation to George Ernst and Elizabeth Backman. To George, owner-manager of the incomparable Shagroy Market in Salisbury, Connecticut, for giving us countless hours of his wise counsel, and his bakery in off hours to launch our empanada enterprise; and to our author's representative, Beth, for her expert advice, for believing there was a book in our empanadas, and, finally, for her determination to see the book realized.

Acknowledgments

We want to thank all the people who gave of their time and/or treasure to launch our empanada venture as a full-time business. Because it always takes courage to commit yourself in the beginning, we especially want to thank Sherry's aunt, Lois Bacon, George's aunt and uncle, John and Ginny Yonkers, Coz Hardee, John Fearnley, Barry Van Kleeck, Albert and Nancy Handy, Susan and Charles Stachelberg, Martha Porter-Terrall, Bob Stetson, Charlotte Reid, Sally Ellsworth, Don and Diane Hewat, Arnold Whitridge, Park Smith, Bud and Chris Trotta, Dick Walsh, Mort Schindel, and Ralph and Ruth Shikes, who advised and supported us from the start. After years of traveling in many parts of this earth, always with one eye out for that special place to call home, we also want to thank the people of the unique northwestern Connecticut towns of Salisbury, Lakeville, Sharon, the Cornwalls, and the Canaans, and The Housatonic Valley Mental Health Center in general, and Dr. Ted Reiss, in particular, for their enthusiasm, encouragement, and support. After all the years of searching, like Dorothy, we know we have finally come home.

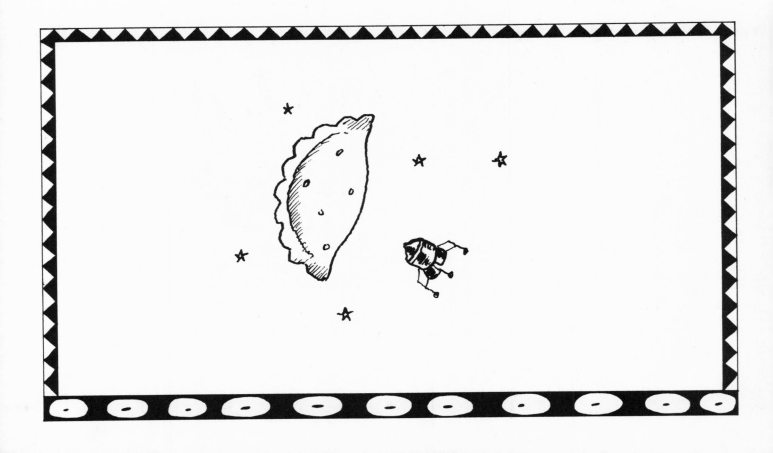

DISCOVERING THE EMPANADA

Em-pan-ada means "that which is covered with bread." In Spanish *pan* is the word for "bread," *ada* translates as "ed," and *em* is the same as the English *im*, therefore, *em-pan-ada* is literally "im-bread-ed."

The empanada, like flamenco dancing, bullfighting, and paella, comes from Spain. We can be certain because in a twelfth-century cathedral honoring Spain's patron Saint James in Santiago de Campostela in the province of Galicia is a statue of a man eating an empanada.

This obviously popular medieval finger food traveled with the Spanish conquistadors to the New World. Here it was adopted by local inhabitants and spread throughout Latin America, from Tierra del Fuego to the Rio Grande.

In countries where Spanish is the native language, you will find empanadas everywhere—in restaurants, in bakeries, at street stands, and in people's homes. This simple baked pastry turnover, with its infinite variety of fillings and its unique ability to add style to any meal from ultra-elegant to everyday, is a natural for today's harassed homemakers—men and women, young and old, Spanish and otherwise, no matter where they happen to reside. Our purpose in writing this book is to raise the empanada consciousness of the non-Spanish-speaking world.

We first encountered empanadas when we were living in Uruguay and Argentina producing documentary films. Our small son was with us, and while we were there, our daughter was born. A *mucama,* or mother's helper, was necessary and Rosita, a large, strong-willed woman, entered our lives. No "little rose" was our Rosita. She was more like La General. Since we were gringos, it was obvious to her that we were ignorant of proper housekeeping, baby care, and food preparation. To salvage the situation La General Rosita took charge of the daily routine in our Buenos Aires apartment. Basic to Rosita's way of life was the empanada. She would arrive each morning with a wicker basket of empanadas on her arm. She would prepare them in our kitchen for lunch and sometimes dinner. She always took them with her when she went to the park with the children. Empanadas were as much a part of her life as her pocketbook or the flaming red lipstick that she chose to wear.

The empanadas always looked the same from the outside: a little puffed brown half-moon of baked pastry completely concealing whatever was inside. The pastry, too, was always the same—light and flaky. It was the filling that was forever different. Whatever was at hand ended up in her empanadas: some leftover meat chopped fine, fruit, vegetables, always garlic or onions, often both, fish, rice, a little cinnamon, salt and pepper, perhaps a splash of wine, or a teaspoon of sugar. Whatever it was, it seemed to come out deliciously different each time.

When the cast and crew for our film project were finally set, we went on location to an old *estancia* (ranch) on the *pampas*. But Rosita, unlike her empanadas, didn't travel well. She refused to leave Buenos Aires. There was an emotional parting. Rosita left us with much hugging, weeping, and a basket full of empanadas. We've never forgotten her.

When we returned to the United States, we continued to prepare and serve and experiment with empanadas. We invented fillings that even Rosita had never discovered. We settled on one pastry dough that is quick and easy to prepare, can take a lot of handling and yet remain elastic, and that produces a light, puffed-up crust every time. We also found new uses for this versatile food. From our experience, Argentines tend to treat their empanadas as a simple, light meal, as we do hamburgers or sandwiches. In this role they are both delicious and nutritious, but they can be much more. By creating a filling such as smoked oysters with chopped eggs and mayonnaise, and then dressing up the pastry with sprigs of fresh parsley and an egg glaze, we can turn the empanada into an elegant hors d'oeuvre. Filled with fruits and other sweets, and dusted with powdered sugar, the empanada becomes a delicious dessert. We also discovered that empanadas are a great convenience food because they store beautifully. We often make up a double batch and freeze them. It's great to know that there is plenty of good nutritious food on call, whenever you may want it.

As we became more involved with empanadas, we discovered that the Spanish were not alone in finding the savory pastry turnover not only a culinary delight but a convenience food as well. The English had their Cornish pasties, which traveled to the British West Indies as Jamaican patties. Then there are the Polish pierogis and the Russian piroshkis, tiny half-moon-shaped turnovers, surrounding distinctly different fillings. Calzone, which means "pants" in Italian, is a pastry turnover filled with a variety of cheese, meats, and spices, literally food in pants. The popular fried snack or appetizer of India and Pakistan is the samosa, little pastry turnovers with savory insides.

Almost without exception the recipes in this book are either our versions of popular empanada fillings, adaptations of other foods to the empanada format, or sheer invention—all the result of years of experimentation with the empanada concept. A preparation time is given with each of our recipes. This includes only the time that you will be physically involved with the food—chopping, mixing, sautéing, whatever. Some ingredients may need to marinate for a number of hours. This doesn't count as preparation time. We don't count baking time either. Once the empanadas are in the oven, you are free until they are ready to come out.

We truly hope that you will enjoy preparing, serving, and eating empanadas. We also hope that you will catch the empanada fever and experiment with some combinations of your own. Just because these filled pastries have been around for more than eight hundred years doesn't mean that there isn't room for innovation and improvement!

BEFORE YOU START

In some restaurants and, more often, street stands in Spain and Latin America, empanadas are fried in deep fat rather than baked in an oven. While the local populations seem to support both cooking methods with equal ardor, we find baking the empanada makes for a much lighter and more delicious food. Our own Quick and Easy Pastry contains only baking ingredients. Also, in many authentic pastry recipes, lard is used as the shortening. In our opinion, this makes for a less digestible and less desirable end product, and we substitute vegetable shortening. You will note that our recipes do not even include salt as an optional ingredient. In view of its possible health hazards, we prefer the more savory and salubrious flavors of herbs and spices. Through the years we have experimented with a number of different pastry recipes, but we think the recipe provided on page 18 is as close to perfection as we will ever get. It is quick and easy to make. The dough is elastic and tolerates a lot of handling without becoming either tough or brittle. It makes a good seal at the seam and it bakes up light and flaky. Once baked, it stores well and freezes beautifully. All of the empanadas and other ethnic pastry turnovers in this book can be made using our Quick and Easy Pastry recipe.

To prepare empanadas you will not need anything that is not normally found in the average kitchen, with one possible exception—an "empanada cutter." All of our snack and entrée empanada recipes are based on a pastry disk 5½ to 6 inches in diameter. In our experience this is the most useful size. A number of ordinary implements are perfectly adequate for cutting these disks. A small saucepan top is perfect if it ends with a vertical edge. The tops of many round plastic refrigerator containers are fine. Even an empty 2-quart juice can or the plastic top from a 3-pound can of shortening or coffee will do. The main thing is to produce a thin pastry disk 5½ to 6 inches in diameter. You should use a smaller disk, such as a 3-inch cookie cutter, when making hors d'oeuvre–size empanadas.

Finally, as with all things, there are tricks to the trade. In making empanadas the tricks are few but necessary. The one thing you must avoid at all costs is a leaky seam. An empanada that spills its insides onto the cookie sheet during baking will burn on the bottom and not be good to eat. Fortunately, the remedial tricks are simple:

- The empanada disks should be filled, edge moistened, and folded as soon as they are cut. They must be elastic to work well. If they dry out, they may break and leak. If, for some reason, you can't fill them all immediately, store them between sheets of waxed paper in the refrigerator, making sure to bring them out to soften at least a half hour before using.
- Make certain that the filling is not of a runny consistency and will stay put. You may abide by this only to discover that your ingredients become more liquid in the oven. Many foods do this. The solution is to include an absorber, like dried fruits or rice, in the filling.
- Don't overfill the pastry. As with any container, if you put more into it than it will naturally hold, it will overflow.
- Once the pastry is filled and folded, make sure that the seam is well closed and crimped. A clean, dry fork does the job nicely.
- Last, a glaze of a beaten whole egg combined with water not only adds a luster to your finished product but helps to seal the surface so that it will be enticingly plump and golden, pleasing to the eye as well as the palate.

Quick and Easy Pastry

Preparation: 10 minutes
Yield: 8 to 10 6-inch or 20 to 25 3-inch disks

¼	pound (1 stick) unsalted butter or margarine (at room temperature)
¼	pound (4 ounces) cream cheese (at room temperature)
1½	cups unbleached flour
½	teaspoon baking powder
1	teaspoon coriander (optional)
¼	teaspoon cider vinegar
2	tablespoons very cold water or milk
1	tablespoon vegetable oil
1	large egg beaten with 2 tablespoons of water (glaze)

1. Preheat oven to 400°.

2. Using a fork, combine the butter or margarine and cream cheese.

3. Sift the flour over this mixture. Add the baking powder, coriander if desired, vinegar, and water or milk and combine with fork.

4. With generously floured hands, work the dough until you have a smooth, resilient ball, 3 to 4 minutes. At first the dough will stick to your fingers, but keep working the flour into the other ingredients until the dough suddenly holds together.

5. Flour both the work surface and your rolling pin, then roll out the pastry dough to about ⅛- to ¹⁄₁₆-inch thickness. Entrée size should be thicker, hors d'oeuvre size thinner. Cut disks the desired size and set aside. When you have cut as many as possible, gather up the scraps and roll out again. Continue this process two or three times until there is not

18

enough left to cut a disk. If you do not have at least 8 entrée or 20 hors d'oeuvre disks, you have not rolled out the pastry thin enough.

6. Oil a large cookie sheet. Spoon 2 tablespoons filling for entrée- or 1 heaping teaspoon for hors d'oeuvre–size empanadas on the disk, making sure the filling is in the center. Moisten the edge of the disk with the egg glaze. Carefully fold the pastry over the filling and crimp the edge seam with a clean, dry fork.

7. Glaze the top of the pastry with the beaten egg mixture. Garnish with herbs or spices suggested in the filling recipes, if desired, and bake in a preheated oven for 10 to 15 minutes for hors d'oeuvre, 15 to 20 minutes for entrée, or until golden brown. Cool on racks.

Note: All of the empanadas that follow can be made in quantity, baked, and frozen in plastic bags for later consumption. To reheat, place frozen empanadas in a 350° oven for approximately 30 minutes. (Do not defrost the empanadas before reheating.)

19

All filling recipes will yield 8 to 10 6-inch empanadas (or 20 to 25 3-inch empanadas if you are preparing hors d'oeuvres).

HORS D'OEUVRES

The literal translation of the French term *hors d'oeuvre* is "outside of the work," meaning something you enjoy before you get down to the serious business of eating. Traditionally, in France, hot hors d'oeuvres were *petit entrées:* miniature versions of the first course—small quiches, soufflés, or croquettes. French chefs let their imaginations run wild creating an almost infinite variety of these little concoctions. In the classic food encyclopedia, *Larousse Gastronomique,* more pages are devoted to hors d'oeuvres than to any other subject. They may be "outside of the work," but a great many French epicures take their hors d'oeuvres seriously.

The French are not alone in this; the Italians have their antipasto, the Chinese their dim sum, the Russians their zakuski, the Polynesians their pau pau, and the Spanish their tapas and their empanadas. These tiny, savory pastry turnovers make almost perfect cocktail finger food. Like a French chef, you can let your imagination abound with the variety of fillings. We like to serve hors d'oeuvre empanadas with red or white wine, cocktails, or, our personal choice, sangria. The following recipes will make 20 to 25 3-inch empanadas.

Baba Gannoujh Empanada

Once upon a time, in Lebanon, there lived a cantankerous old widower. He had one doting daughter and no teeth. Every day the daughter would bake eggplant, mash the pulp with other ingredients, chill it, and feed it to the old man. Neighbors and friends tried to explain that her father was perfectly capable of consuming other soft foods, but the daughter would not listen. By the time he died, she had beome so accustomed to preparing it that she continued to do so. She ate it herself and served it to all her neighbors and relatives, who named it baba gannoujh, "spoiled old papa" in Lebanese.

In our opinion, "spoiled old papa" makes an unusually delicious hors d'oeuvre empanada filling.

Preparation: 15 minutes

1	large eggplant
3	tablespoons finely chopped onion
2	tablespoons olive oil
2	tablespoons fresh lemon juice
1	teaspoon coriander
1/4	teaspoon cumin
1/4	cup chopped fresh parsley
	Freshly ground white pepper to taste
	Garnish: Dried parsley or dillweed, paprika

1. Bake eggplant 1 hour at 350° or until cooked through. Cool and set aside.

2. When the eggplant is cool enough to handle, cut in half and scoop out pulp with a spoon into a small mixing bowl. Discard skin.

3. Add remaining ingredients and mash together.

4. Now you are ready to roll out and fill disks. Sprinkle the garnish, if desired, on top of the final egg glaze.

22

Chicken Liver Pâté Empanada

A true French pâté is, by definition, a "cubic" cousin to the empanada—a pastry case filled with prepared meats, fish, or vegetables. French pâtés, however, are much larger than empanadas, are baked in a mold, which is usually rectangular, and are sliced for serving.

In the United States the term pâté *often refers only to the filling, chicken liver being one of the most popular types. Here is our chicken liver version for filling empanadas. Actually almost any pâté filling can be used to stuff an empanada, with the exception of those that contain pork, which requires a longer cooking time than empanadas.*

Preparation: 15 minutes

1/4 cup unsalted butter or margarine
1/2 pound chicken livers
3 tablespoons chopped yellow onion
1 teaspoon rosemary
1 tablespoon Dijon mustard
1 tablespoon lemon juice
1 tablespoon grated lemon rind
2 tablespoons cognac or brandy
Freshly ground black pepper to taste

1. Heat butter or margarine and sauté the chicken livers and onions over a moderately high flame until tender, about 3 minutes. Place in a blender or food processor and add the rosemary, mustard, lemon juice, rind, and cognac or brandy. Blend about 30 seconds or until smooth. Season to taste.

2. Now you are ready to roll out and fill disks.

Coquilles St. Jacques Empanada

A friend of Sherry's, a Wall Street attorney, retired some years ago to become a Nantucket scallop fisherman. Although he sold most of his catch (after all, it was a business), he always reserved some of the succulent shellfish for friends. Through his generosity, we have enjoyed scallops fried, sautéed, broiled, and kebabed, but our favorite is coquilles St. Jacques. It makes a particularly delicious hors d'oeuvre empanada.

Preparation: 15 minutes

1/2 pound bay scallops, sliced in half
1/2 cup dry vermouth or white wine
2   tablespoons unsalted butter or margarine
2   tablespoons shallots, minced
2   cloves garlic, minced
2   tablespoons flour
1/2 cup sour cream or plain yogurt
    Freshly grated Parmesan cheese to taste
    Pinch dried thyme
    Freshly ground black pepper to taste
    Garnish: Paprika

1. Simmer scallops in vermouth or wine for 3 minutes. Drain, reserving liquid, and set aside.

2. Melt butter or margarine, and sauté shallots and garlic until golden, not brown, about 1 minute.

3. Sprinkle flour over shallots and stir quickly until it forms a thick paste. Add reserved wine and sour cream or yogurt, stirring until smooth. Add Parmesan cheese, thyme, and pepper. Combine mixture with scallops.

4. Now you are ready to roll out and fill disks. Sprinkle the garnish on top of the final egg glaze, and bake as directed.

French Rissole

Rissoles have a documented history almost as old as that of empanadas. Originally a pancake wrapped around whatever food was available, sealed at the edges, fried, and eaten out of hand, they were known in thirteenth-century Paris as the workingman's supper. Over the centuries, rissoles left the arena of street food, shrank in size, acquired epicurean fillings, and entered the realm of fashion as elegant hors d'oeuvres. Recipes for rissoles often contain such esoteric ingredients as cock's combs, sweetbreads, brains, and more often than almost any other ingredient, truffles and foie gras. This recipe is our adaptation just in case you don't happen to have a ready supply of truffles and foie gras.

Preparation: 30 minutes

1	cup chopped onion
2	tablespoons unsalted butter
¼	cup chicken stock
¼	pound pâté de foie gras or chicken liver pâté
2	cups truffles or chopped mushrooms
	Freshly ground black pepper to taste

1. Sauté onion in butter until golden. Add chicken stock and pâté. Combine well and heat through.

2. Add truffles or mushrooms. Sauté briefly until heated through, stirring to combine well. Add pepper to taste and let cool.

3. Now you are ready to roll out and fill disks.

25

Ham and Artichoke Heart Empanada

We have often heard that it must have been a very brave, or very hungry, person who first ate an oyster. We think it must be equally true of the first person who ate an artichoke.

A gigantic member of the thistle family, artichokes do not present themselves as obvious epicurean delights. Their very name is enough to give one pause. If you have ever had the misfortune to swallow the thistle or "choke" part, you will know how apt the name is. However, tinned artichoke hearts, from very young plants, are delicious. Their delicate flavor coupled with the more robust ham, plus the pungent addition of Dijon mustard, makes for a delightful combination.

Preparation: 20 minutes

8   canned marinated artichoke hearts, drained
1   cup diced cooked ham
2   tablespoons Dijon mustard
1   cup plain yogurt
1   tablespoon dillweed
    Garnish: Paprika, dried parsley

1. Chop artichoke hearts and combine with ham, mustard, yogurt, and dillweed.

2. Now you are ready to roll out and fill disks. Sprinkle the garnish, if desired, on top of the final egg glaze.

Humos Bi Tahini Empanada

Humos bi tahini, *a paste of chickpeas and sesame seeds, is an ancient and still popular Middle Eastern dish. Both ingredients are naturally abundant throughout North Africa and the Middle East to central Asia. Humos bi tahini is usually served in the pocket of a half-round of pita bread. The result is not unlike an open-ended empanada.*

Chickpeas, or as the Spanish call them, garbanzos, *came to America with empanadas and the conquistadors in the sixteenth-century. Sesame seeds, called* bennes, *came over with African slaves a hundred years later. But Americans never put the two together until immigrants from the Middle East brought* humos bi tahini *with them in the nineteenth-century.*

Preparation: 20 minutes

- 1   20-ounce can chickpeas, rinsed and drained
- 1   cup tahini (ground sesame seeds)
- 2   large cloves garlic
- 3/4 cup fresh lemon juice
- 1/2 cup chopped fresh parsley
- 1 1/2 cups light salad oil
- 1   tablespoon coriander
    Freshly ground black pepper to taste
- 1   large ripe tomato or 6 cherry tomatoes, chopped

1. Place chickpeas, tahini, garlic, lemon juice, parsley, oil, and coriander in blender or food processor and blend until smooth, about 30 seconds. Add freshly ground pepper to taste. Add chopped tomato. Combine well.

2. Now you are ready to roll out and fill disks.

27

Oriental Seafood Empanada à la Yuriko

Many years ago, George had the good fortune to live next door to Yuriko, a former dancer with Martha Graham, who now heads a distinguished company of her own, and her husband, Charlie Kikuchi. They introduced him to the delicious possibilities of cold marinated seafood and rice served with a variety of Oriental condiments. Over the years we prepared similar dishes, changing some ingredients and adding others, until we arrived at the following recipe. A kaleidoscope of bright red, green, and white, this salad is a feast for the eyes, as well as for the palate, and it makes an exquisite hors d'oeuvre empanada.

Preparation: 30 minutes

1	cup cooked rice
1/2	cup sliced water chestnuts
1/2	cup chopped celery
1/2	cup sliced fresh mushrooms
1/2	cup chopped green pepper
1/2	cup chopped scallions, including green part
3	ounces lobster meat or frozen *langostinos* (salt-water crayfish)
3	ounces medium-size shrimp
3	ounces king crab meat
1/2	cup soy or safflower oil
2	tablespoons fresh lemon juice
1	tablespoon dark soy sauce
1	tablespoon Dijon mustard
1	tablespoon brown sugar
1	teaspoon ground ginger (or to taste)
	Freshly ground black pepper to taste
	Garnish: Dried parsley or dillweed, paprika

1. Combine rice with water chestnuts, celery, mushrooms, green pepper, and scallions.

2. Place the seafood in a pot with enough boiling water to cover. When water comes to a second boil, drain the seafood, chop, and add to rice and chopped vegetables. *Do not overcook!*

3. Mix the dressing of oil, lemon juice, soy sauce, mustard, brown sugar, ginger, and pepper to taste.

4. Add the dressing to the rice-vegetable-seafood mixture and toss. Refrigerate 4 to 5 hours or even overnight, tossing several times.

5. Now you are ready to roll out and fill disks. Sprinkle garnish on top of final egg glaze, if desired.

Pâté Edith Empanada

Sherry created this delicious vegetarian pâté for our good friend and neighbor to serve at an impromptu cocktail party. It looks and tastes remarkably like a meat pâté, and it fooled most of the guests at the party. The secret is walnuts and Worcestershire sauce. We think it makes a tasty filling for empanadas. Also, unlike any other pâté we know of, it freezes superbly, so you might want to make extra to keep on hand.

Preparation: 15 minutes

1	cup walnuts
1	6-ounce can black California pitted olives, drained
8	ounces cream cheese
10	ounces mozzarella cheese, grated
4 to 6	tablespoons Worcestershire sauce (as desired for taste and color)
1	tablespoon cognac
1/4	cup chopped fresh parsley
	Several twists freshly ground pepper
1/3	cup chopped walnuts

1. With steel blade of food processor, process 1 cup walnuts until fine. Remove from processor.

2. Combine all other ingredients with ground walnuts until smooth and delicate.

3. Add 1/3 cup chopped walnuts and combine well.

4. Now you are ready to roll out and fill disks.

Shrimp and Water Chestnut Empanada

Although this empanada sounds as if it must have Chinese roots, it really doesn't. It is pure invention. We selected a number of varied ingredients that, in our opinion, were compatible. We juggled them around, adding a bit here, subtracting there, until we came up with the following recipe. It is truly an international empanada reaching out to Asian, Slavic, Latin, and Anglo sources for its ingredients.

Preparation: 25 minutes

- ³/₄ cup cooked tiny Alaskan shrimp or minced cooked medium-size shrimp
- ³/₄ cup chopped water chestnuts
- ¹/₃ cup sour cream or plain yogurt
- 1 tablespoon tomato purée
- 2 tablespoons dry sherry
- 1 teaspoon chopped fresh chives
- 1 teaspoon chopped fresh parsley
- 1 teaspoon dillweed
- 1 clove garlic, minced
  Freshly ground black pepper to taste
  Garnish: Paprika

1. Combine all ingredients. Season to taste.

2. Now you are ready to roll out and fill disks. Sprinkle the garnish, if desired, on top of the final egg glaze.

31

Russian Piroshki

Serve empanadas in Moscow or piroshki in Madrid and no one would consider anything amiss, since piroshki, the Russian cocktail-size empanada, is so similar to its Latin cousin. The Russians have one advantage, however. During their long cold winters, large batches of piroshkis can be made, placed on a window ledge facing north, and frozen for future use.

In Russia, piroshkis usually accompany a soup, or they may be served as part of the zakuski *(Russian hors d'oeuvres) and washed down with a tiny glass of vodka, consumed in one swallow.*

The following recipe is for the beef-and-chopped-egg piroshki.

Preparation: 25 minutes

2	tablespoons unsalted butter or margarine
1	large yellow onion, minced
1	pound ground lean beef
1/2	cup sour cream
1	tablespoon dillweed
3	hard-boiled eggs, chopped
1/2	teaspoon freshly ground black pepper

1. Melt butter or margarine in a skillet, add onion and sauté gently until transparent.

2. Add the beef and cook until browned. Drain off fat.

3. Add the other ingredients and cook briefly, 2 to 3 minutes.

4. Now you are ready to roll out and fill disks.

Polish Pierogi

Polish pierogis are small empanada-shaped pastry turnovers usually filled with cabbage, onions, herbs, and sometimes chopped beef or fish. Pierogis can be baked, fried, or even boiled and used as dumplings in soups. In fact, in Polish, pierogi can also mean "dumpling." Pierogis are usually associated with the soup dish, although they can certainly be served as an hors d'oeuvre as well.

This recipe is for the classic Polish cabbage-and-onion pierogi.

Preparation: 20 minutes

2 tablespoons unsalted butter or margarine
2 large yellow onions, chopped
5 cups boiled and chopped green cabbage
2 hard-boiled eggs, chopped
1 tablespoon chopped fresh parsley

1. Melt butter or margarine and sauté the onions until lightly browned.

2. Add all the other ingredients and sauté briefly until thoroughly combined and warmed through, 2 or 3 minutes. Do not overcook.

3. Now you are ready to roll out and fill disks.

Smoked Oyster Empanada

There are certain foods that most kids won't eat. From our experience, mushrooms and oysters top the list. Smoked oysters, however, are something special.

One of the advantages of the empanada is that, unless you are told, you have no way of knowing what's inside. So, do your kids a favor and serve them smoked oyster empanadas without telling. Chances are they will become converts for life. Smoked oyster empanadas also are quite popular with adults.

Preparation: 25 minutes

3	hard-boiled eggs, chopped
2/3	cup mayonnaise (preferably homemade)
2	tablespoons Dijon mustard
	Freshly ground black pepper to taste
2	10-ounce cans smoked oysters
	Garnish: Dried parsley, paprika

1. Combine chopped eggs, mayonnaise, mustard, and pepper. Mix to a uniform consistency.

2. Roll out and cut disks.

3. Place about 1 teaspoon of the egg mixture in the center of the pastry disk, add 1 oyster, fold over and crimp pastry with a fork.

4. Glaze with egg and garnish with parsley and a sprinkling of paprika. Bake as directed.

Spanish Tapa de Atun Empanada *(Tuna Empanada)*

The Spanish, in general, eat their evening meal when most Americans are watching the eleven o'clock news. The reason for this is the sacred siesta, or afternoon nap, when all but essential work stops. In Madrid, offices don't usually close until after 7:30 P.M. Since the evening meal is still a few hours away, this is tapas *time, when bars and cafés serve a remarkable variety of these hearty hors d'oeuvres to hungry people.*

It was in a café in Madrid, while drinking wine and sampling tapas, *that we enjoyed this* tapa de atun.

▲▲▲▲▲▲▲▲▲▲▲▲▲▲▲▲▲▲▲▲▲▲▲▲▲▲▲▲▲▲▲

Preparation: 15 minutes

2	tablespoons olive oil
3	large cloves garlic, minced
$1/2$	pound fresh tuna, mako shark, or swordfish, cubed
	Juice of 2 lemons
$1/3$	cup mayonnaise (preferably homemade)
$1/2$	teaspoon dried mustard
$1/4$	cup chopped fresh parsley
	Freshly ground black pepper to taste

1. Heat olive oil and sauté garlic briefly until just wilted.

2. Add tuna and lemon juice and sauté over moderate heat until cooked through, 6 to 8 minutes.

3. Combine tuna mixture in a bowl with mayonnaise, mustard, and parsley. Season to taste. Now you are ready to roll out and fill disks.

Note: Canned tuna may be substituted for fresh fish if absolutely necessary.

SNACKS AND LIGHT LUNCHES

Today the most popular light lunch or snack in the United States is, undoubtedly, the sandwich. It was invented by John Montague, the fourth earl of Sandwich, a town on the coast of England. The earl was very fond of gambling and he would not leave the gaming table, even to take food, if the stakes were high. Instead, he would order his servants to bring him slices of roast meat between two pieces of bread. Thus was born the sandwich.

To the west of Sandwich, along the Cornish coast, other less well-heeled Englishmen were carrying their lunch to work in the mines. This lunch was a Cornish pastie, hearty food wrapped up in a sealed pastry pouch. In other parts of the world other workingmen were carrying similar meals with them and had been for centuries. Called pastie, calzone, or empanada, this turnover still makes a perfect snack or light lunch for today's mobile population. We generally serve crudités, or cut-up raw vegetables, along with our snack or light luncheon empanadas. These recipes will fill 8 to 10 6-inch empanadas.

Ham and Spiced Apple Empanada

In the good old days a roast suckling pig, served with an apple in its mouth, was a traditional dish for the festive Christmas and New Year's holiday season. Pork and apples just naturally go together. For an empanada we had to be a bit less grandiose in our concept. Diced ham and apples spiced with brown sugar and cloves and resting in a bed of sour cream makes a festive dish for any occasion, or even for no occasion at all. A satisfying snack or light lunch, this also serves as a tempting hors d'oeuvre.

Preparation: 15 minutes

1/2   cup sour cream or plain yogurt
1/4   teaspoon ground cloves
2   teaspoons brown sugar
1/2   cup chopped dried apple slices
1   cup cubed cooked ham

1. Combine all ingredients.

2. Now you are ready to roll out and fill disks.

Egyptian Falafel Empanada

We had just completed shooting a film on the construction of the Aswan Dam and were in Karnak visiting the incredible Egyptian ruins. In the garden of a Victorian English hotel we were served this refreshing and satisfying combination of unlikely ingredients: chickpeas, bulgur wheat, tomatoes, cucumbers, garlic, and spices. Although it sounds like a salad, traditionally it is formed into balls and sautéed like hamburgers. Falafel is strange, exotic, and delicious. We think it makes an unusually good empanada filling.

Preparation: 25 minutes

1	cup bulgur wheat
1	cup cooked garbanzos or chickpeas
1	cup black olives, pitted and sliced
1	cucumber, peeled, diced, and seeded
1/4	cup sesame seeds
1/2	cup red or green peppers, diced
1/4	cup fresh lemon juice
2	large cloves garlic, minced
1	tablespoon mint flakes
1	teaspoon coriander
1 1/2	tablespoons chili powder

1. Cover bulgur wheat with boiling water and let stand 30 minutes. The water will be absorbed by the bulgur wheat.

2. Purée garbanzos in food processor or blender.

3. Combine all ingredients and let marry for at least 30 minutes.

4. Now you are ready to roll out and fill disks.

39

Egg Roll Empanada

As soon as we are seated in a Chinese restaurant the first thing our family orders is egg rolls. We've tried, but we've never been able to duplicate that bubbly, crisp, fried crust in our own kitchen. However, we can wrap that delicious Oriental mix of tastes and textures up in an empanada and enjoy a slightly different, but equally delicious, eating experience. A perfect light lunch, they are also good as an hors d'oeuvre.

Preparation: 20 minutes

- ¼ cup soy sauce
- ⅓ cup chopped celery
- ½ cup chopped cabbage (preferably Chinese cabbage)
- ½ cup diced cooked shrimp
- ⅓ cup diced cooked pork or ham
- ⅓ cup diced water chestnuts
- 1 large clove garlic, finely minced
- 2 teaspoons minced fresh chives or scallions (green part)
- 1 tablespoon hot Chinese mustard
- 3 tablespoons apricot jam

1. Place all ingredients in a bowl and toss like a salad to distribute soy sauce and mix the ingredients. Let rest at least an hour (overnight in the refrigerator is fine) in order for ingredients to marry.

2. Now you are ready to roll out and fill disks.

Granola Empanada

This is the anytime, anyplace empanada. Packed with dried fruit, nuts, and rolled oats, and using honey as a binder, it is perfect for snacking either at home or on the trail. It will stay fresh and delicious for a couple of days without refrigeration. Any combination of dried fruits and nuts can be used; this just happens to be our favorite. It is also good for breakfast.

Preparation: 10 minutes

¹/₂	cup quick-rolled oats
2	tablespoons dried currants
2	tablespoons chopped dried apricots
2	tablespoons chopped dried apples
2	tablespoons slivered almonds
¹/₃	cup honey
1	cup applesauce

1. Combine oats with currants, apricots, apples, and almonds. Combine honey and applesauce with dry ingredients and mix well.

2. Now you are ready to roll out and fill disks.

Guacamole Empanada

Give ten avocados to ten Mexican chefs and you'll have ten different versions of this famous south-of-the-border dip. We'll give you an eleventh. Substituting red bell peppers, cauliflower, and broccoli florets for the usual chopped tomatoes gives the guacamole texture and makes this an out-of-the-ordinary luncheon empanada.

Preparation: 15 minutes

3	large garlic cloves
4	tablespoons chopped yellow onion
4 to 5	large ripe avocados
1	tablespoon hot green chili pepper, chopped fine
2	tablespoons coriander
1	teaspoon cumin powder
1/4	cup fresh lemon juice
1/2	cup mayonnaise (preferably homemade)
1	cup coarsely chopped fresh cauliflower florets
1	cup coarsely chopped fresh broccoli florets
1/2	cup chopped red bell peppers

1. Mince garlic and chop onion in a wooden bowl. With a fork, mash until garlic and onion juices flow.

2. Cut avocados in half, remove pits, and with a spoon scoop out all the flesh into the bowl with the mashed onion and garlic, and combine with other ingredients.

3. Now you are ready to roll out and fill disks.

Italian Calzone

Besides being a real old-fashioned place that serves delicious pizza, our local pizzeria is memorable because it also offers calzone, the Italian version of an empanada. Calzones are always filled with a combination of cheeses plus a variety of meats and herbs. This is our favorite blend.

Preparation: 15 minutes

1   cup ricotta cheese
1/4   cup grated Parmesan cheese
1/4   pound mozzarella cheese, cubed
1/4   pound hot Italian sausage or
       pepperoni, sliced and quartered
1/4   pound prosciutto (or smoked ham),
       cubed
1   tablespoon oregano
1   tablespoon chopped fresh parsley
1   teaspoon freshly ground pepper

1. Combine all ingredients and mix thoroughly.

2. Now you are ready to roll out and fill disks.

Mussels à la Marinière Empanada

All over the world people relish this common, nutritious shellfish, the mussel . . . all over the world, except in the United States. We hope to win a few converts with this simple recipe. And if the filling doesn't do it, perhaps the price will. Mussels are one of the least expensive foods that you can buy.

Preparation: 10 minutes

2 8-ounce cans of mussels, drained
3/4 cup fresh lemon juice
3 teaspoons Dijon mustard
2 tablespoons minced shallots
3/4 cup instant rice
Freshly ground black pepper to taste

1. Combine all the ingredients and let rest for 20 to 30 minutes, or until all liquid is absorbed by the rice. Stir once or twice, if necessary.

2. Now you are ready to roll out and fill disks.

Ratatouille Empanada

Ratatouille is a country specialty from the south of France, where it has been a basic food for centuries. We always add grated cheese to ratatouille. It makes for a nice taste and textural contrast to the vegetables. Served with a glass of wine or beer, a ratatouille empanada is a well-balanced and satisfying vegetarian lunch.

Preparation: 30 minutes

- 1/3 cup of soy, safflower, or olive oil
- 2 cloves garlic, minced
- 1/2 Bermuda onion, thinly sliced
- 2 small zucchini, cubed
- 1/2 cup flour
- 1 green pepper, diced
- 1 cup tomato purée
- 1 tablespoon dried basil
- 1 tablespoon capers
- 1/4 cup chopped fresh parsley
- 1/4 pound Swiss or mozzarella cheese, freshly grated
  Freshly ground black pepper to taste
  Garnish: Dried parsley or dillweed, paprika

1. Heat oil in a large, heavy skillet or casserole dish and add garlic and onion. Sauté gently until transparent.

2. Sprinkle zucchini with flour, add to the casserole, and cook gently for about 5 minutes.

3. Add the green pepper, tomato purée, basil, capers, parsley, cheese, and pepper to taste. Cook through for about 3 minutes. Cool.

4. Now you are ready to roll out and fill disks. Sprinkle garnish on pastry after final egg glaze, if desired.

Papas Sabrosas Empanada

We always assumed potatoes came from Ireland, Russia, or some other place in Europe until we lived in South America, the original home of this ubiquitous tuber. Papa Sabrosa means "savory potato," and this is just what an old man with a pushcart used to sell to us when we lived on the outskirts of Montevideo, Uruguay. This is a simple, down-to-basics, empanada that makes a satisfying lunch and is one of our children's favorites.

Preparation: 15 minutes

1   cup leftover mashed or diced boiled potatoes
2   tablespoons tomato purée
1/2   cup sour cream or plain yogurt
1/3   cup chopped scallions, including green part
1/2   cup grated sharp Cheddar cheese
1/3   cup minced ham (optional)
    Freshly ground black pepper to taste
    Garnish: Dried parsley or dillweed

1. Combine all ingredients and season to taste.

2. Now you are ready to roll out and fill disks. Sprinkle garnish on pastry after final egg glaze, if desired.

Pizza Empanada

This recipe is for a basic cheese-and-salami-pizza empanada. You can let your imagination run wild with olives, anchovies, mushrooms, ham, sausage—almost anything is possible. It's also great for family meals. Involve the kids, and let each one create his or her favorite.

Preparation: 20 minutes

1/3	cup tomato purée
2	teaspoons oregano
1	clove garlic, minced
	Freshly ground black pepper to taste
5	slices hard salami, halved
1/2	cup cooked sausage, chopped olives, anchovies, mushrooms, or cooked ham, or any combination (optional)
1/2	cup grated mozzarella cheese

1. Roll out dough and cut disks.

2. Combine tomato purée, oregano, and minced garlic. Add pepper to taste.

3. Place salami half on disk, along with any optional ingredients, if desired. Spread with tomato sauce, top with mozzarella, fold over and crimp the pastry with a fork.

4. Glaze with egg and bake as directed.

Nancy's Sweet Potatoes Supreme Empanada

This recipe was given to us by an old friend whose parents came from Virginia. A dish with a southern drawl, it makes a sweet and satisfying light vegetarian lunch, or a special side dish with ham or chicken on a cold winter's night.

Preparation: 20 minutes

6	medium sweet potatoes or yams
	A few drops of salad oil
4	eggs
1/4	cup unsalted butter or margarine
1	teaspoon cinnamon
1/4	cup undiluted frozen orange juice concentrate
1	8½-ounce can crushed pineapple, drained
1	cup raisins
1/8	cup rum or bourbon

1. Preheat oven to 350°.

2. Rub the potato skins with oil and bake for 1 hour. When cool, slip potatoes out of their skins and chop.

3. Combine with remaining ingredients.

4. Now you are ready to roll out and fill disks.

Sweet and Sour Pork Empanada

Our children are not big on experimentation when it comes to foreign food. In a Chinese restaurant, after the egg rolls, they invariably order sweet and sour pork, an American favorite. To mix things up further, we've also wrapped it up as an empanada. It is very easy to prepare and will serve as a special snack or light lunch. It also makes a very tasty hors d'oeuvre.

Preparation: 15 minutes

¼ cup soy sauce
¼ cup brown sugar
½ teaspoon chopped fresh ginger
1 teaspoon dry mustard
½ cup chopped dried apricots
1 cup diced cooked lean pork or ham

1. Combine soy sauce, brown sugar, ginger, and mustard. Add apricots and pork or ham. Let ingredients marinate together for at least 1 hour (overnight in the refrigerator is fine).

2. Now you are ready to roll out and fill disks.

Spinach and Feta Cheese Empanada

The Greeks have a word for it—spanakopita. Their triangular puff pastry pies, filled with chopped spinach and feta cheese, are delicious. With more filling and less pastry, however, we've got a new name for it—empanada. These make a delicious light vegetarian lunch, and they are equally good in the smaller hors d'oeuvre size.

This spinach and feta cheese empanada has consistently been the most popular of all the varieties we sell in retail markets. In fact, these empanadas were served at former New York Governor Hugh Carey's wedding reception in 1981.

Preparation: 20 minutes

- 1 cup crumbled feta cheese
- 1 10-ounce package frozen chopped spinach, defrosted and well drained
- 1 cup shredded mozzarella cheese
- ¼ cup commercial all-natural mayonnaise or homemade
- ¼ cup plain yogurt
- 1 tablespoon dried dillweed
- 1 tablespoon Dijon mustard
- 1 teaspoon oregano
  Freshly ground black pepper to taste
  Garnish: Dried dillweed or parsley, paprika

1. Combine all ingredients. Season with black pepper to taste.

2. Now you are ready to roll out and fill disks. Sprinkle with garnish, if desired, after final egg glaze.

50

Peruvian Empanadas

Potatoes are native to South America and were first cultivated by Andean Indians on the high plateau where it is too cold to raise corn. Although quite uncommon once, potatoes have now become one of the basic foods of the world. They are mashed, puréed, riced, and sliced. So, how about doing something unique with the old tuber? In an empanada shell they make a satisfying vegetarian lunch.

Preparation: 10 minutes

4	cups of cooked, cubed, peeled potatoes (canned will do)
1/2	cup cottage cheese
1	cup chopped celery
1/2	cup shredded mozzarella cheese
1/2	cup shredded sharp Cheddar cheese
1/3	cup chopped fresh parsley
2	tablespoons Dijon mustard
	Pinch thyme
	Freshly ground pepper to taste
1/4 to 1/2	cup instant rice

1. Combine all ingredients plus ¼ cup rice, and let stand for about 20 minutes. If mixture seems too liquid, add another ¼ cup instant rice.

2. Now you are ready to roll out and fill disks.

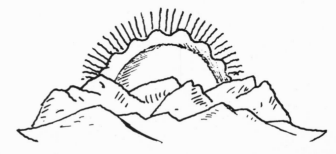

ENTRÉES

Entrée in French means "the entering," or first course at a formal dinner (excluding hors d'oeuvres, soups, and fish). Although there were often many entrées in the grand old days of dining, today entrée implies the main course, no matter where it comes in the meal.

The entrée empanada recipes that follow are hearty main-course foods. If you want a taste of the good old days, you can, at different times, make up a number of different kinds of empanadas, freeze them, and then serve some of each at future dinners. We often do this. It gives your guests options, allows them to savor different tastes, and adds variety to your entrée course. After all, variety was what the French formal dinner was all about.

Depending upon the season, we generally serve our 6-inch entrée empanadas with hot or cold soup and a fresh garden salad or vegetable casserole. Because of the rich pastry shell, in the summer we generally have some kind of sorbet (like a sherbet but without milk or cream) for dessert; in the winter, crème caramel, gingerbread, or mousse au chocolat.

Argentine Spiced Beef Empanada

This was the first empanada recipe we wrote as our own. It is also the recipe that won the Woman's Day Silver Spoon Award for creative cookery for Sherry.

Our Argentine spiced beef empanada is obviously influenced by its heritage, yet the blend of ingredients is unique. It may be the oldest, but it's still our family favorite. It's a crowd pleaser too; everyody likes its sweet and spicy combination of ingredients.

Preparation: 30 minutes

3	tablespoons unsalted butter or margarine
1/3	cup chopped yellow onion
1/2	pound ground chopped beef
1/3	cup currants
2	tablespoons slivered almonds
1	teaspoon ground cinnamon
2	teaspoons chili powder
3	tablespoons brown sugar
1	large egg, lightly beaten
	Freshly ground black pepper to taste

1. Heat butter and sauté chopped onion until golden, about 1 to 2 minutes. With slotted spoon or spatula remove onion and place in a medium-size mixing bowl.

2. Sauté beef in remaining butter over moderate flame until cooked through, about 3 minutes. Place in bowl with onion. Add remaining ingredients and mix well. Season to taste.

3. Now you are ready to roll out and fill disks.

Note: If mixture appears dry, add a little red wine or beef bouillon to moisten before filling pastry.

Argentine Empanadas de Horno *(Baked Empanadas)*

About a block and a half from our apartment in Buenos Aires, there was a bakery that offered, along with their usual goods, a variety of empanadas. They were baked twice a day and were usually warm. At noon and after working hours, the stock of empanadas would rapidly disappear as people bought this convenient, tasty, and wholesome light lunch or predinner snack. Since this was a bakery, they were called empanadas de horno, horno being Spanish for "oven." There were always at least three varieties: chicken (below), meat, and cheese (following pages).

Pollo *(Chicken)* Filling

Preparation: 20 minutes

1	tablespoon unsalted butter
1	tablespoon olive oil
1/2	cup minced yellow onion
1	cup diced cooked chicken
1/2	cup diced green pepper
2	ripe plum tomatoes, peeled, seeded, and finely chopped (or canned)
	Juice and grated rind of 1 lemon
1	3-ounce tin anchovies, drained and chopped (optional)
1/3	cup dry red wine
	Freshly ground black pepper to taste

1. Melt butter in skillet, add olive oil, and sauté onion until just wilted, 1 to 2 minutes.

2. Combine all other ingredients except the pepper, and cook over moderate heat, stirring occasionally, for about 10 minutes. Add pepper to taste.

3. Now you are ready to roll out and fill disks.

Carne *(Meat)* Filling

Preparation: 15 minutes

2	tablespoons olive oil
1/2	cup chopped yellow onion
1/2	pound sirloin steak, cubed
	Flour for dusting steak
1/2	cup diced fresh or drained canned peaches
1	teaspoon seeded and crumbled dried chili pepper
1/2	teaspoon paprika
1/4	teaspoon ground cumin
	Freshly ground black pepper to taste

1. Heat olive oil and sauté chopped onion over moderate heat until just wilted, 1 to 2 minutes.

2. Dust steak with flour, combine with onions, and continue cooking over moderate heat until cooked through, 8 to 10 minutes.

3. Put meat and onions in a medium-size bowl and add the peaches, chili pepper, paprika, cumin, and pepper to taste.

4. Now you are ready to roll out and fill disks.

Jamón y Queso *(Ham and Cheese)* Filling

Preparation: 15 minutes

- 2 tablespoons olive oil
- 1/2 cup chopped yellow onion
- 1 clove garlic, minced
- 1/2 cup cubed top-quality ham
- 1/2 cup shredded sharp Cheddar cheese
- 1/4 teaspoon chili powder
- 8 to 10 pimiento-stuffed green olives

1. Heat olive oil and sauté onion and garlic over moderate heat until just wilted, 1 to 2 minutes.

2. Combine onion and garlic with the ham, cheese, and chili powder in a medium-size bowl and mix thoroughly.

3. Roll out dough and fill disks as directed. Place one stuffed olive in the center of the filling before folding over and crimping.

Beef Stroganoff Empanada

Every Russian restaurant worth its beluga caviar will offer beef Stroganoff on the menu. Of course, another place where you can enjoy is in your own home. If you just happen to have some left over, add a little sour cream or plain yogurt to make a delicious empanada filling. If you don't have any leftover Stroganoff, here is a recipe just right for filling 8 to 10 entrée empanadas.

Preparation: 30 minutes

- 4 tablespoons unsalted butter or margarine
- 3/4 pound sirloin steak, all excess fat and gristle removed
- 2 tablespoons shallots, minced
- 2 tablespoons flour
- 3/4 cup beef broth
- 1 cup sour cream, or a mix of 1/2 cup sour cream and 1/2 cup yogurt
- 1 tablespoon Dijon mustard
- 1 tablespoon capers
- 1/4 pound fresh mushrooms, sliced
  Freshly ground black pepper to taste

1. Heat butter or margarine in a large skillet over medium high heat. Add meat and sauté, very quickly, about 1 to 2 minutes per side. Remove to cutting board and slice into strips about 1/4 inch thick and 1 inch long. Set aside.

2. Pour out all but about 2 tablespoons of fat in skillet and sauté shallots over moderate heat for about 30 seconds. Add flour and beat with a wire whisk until a thick paste is formed. Gradually add the broth until the sauce is smooth and creamy.

3. Turn heat to low and add remaining ingredients. Continue to stir until smooth and heated through. Cool.

4. Now you are ready to roll out and fill disks.

Chicken Polynesian Empanada

Because of all the tropical fruit this recipe contains, it makes a refreshing "tailgate" or summer picnic empanada.

Preparation: 20 minutes

1	cup slivered cooked chicken
1	8½-ounce can of diced pineapple, drained and chopped
2	oranges, chopped in ½-inch pieces
2	bananas, chopped in ½-inch pieces
4	tablespoons unsalted butter or margarine
½	cup almonds, sautéed in 4 tablespoons butter or margarine and drained on paper towels
½	cup shredded coconut
1	Bermuda onion, thinly sliced
½	cup minced crystallized ginger
2	teaspoons cinnamon
1	teaspoon coriander
¼	teaspoon nutmeg
1	cup plain yogurt
½ to 1	cup instant rice

1. Combine all ingredients plus ½ cup rice. Let rest for 30 minutes. If filling seems too liquid, add remaining ½ cup of rice and let stand 15 minutes more.

2. Now you are ready to roll out and fill disks.

Bastard Beef Wellington Empanada

Beef Wellington is one of those exceptional dishes usually served only in a few first-class hotels and aboard luxury liners. It is expensive and complicated, but appealing to both the eye and the palate. We call ours "bastard beef Wellington" because we substitute a well-marinated (4 or 5 days) round steak for the high-priced tenderloin filet and either Chicken Liver Pâté or Pâté Edith for the even more expensive pâté de foie gras that normally caps the filet. This is a very special entrée empanada filling.

Preparation: 30 minutes

1¹/₂ pounds round steak, trimmed of all
       fat
4   tablespoons unsalted butter or
       margarine
2   tablespoons shallots, minced
2   tablespoons flour
1   cup Chicken Liver Pâté (page 23) or
       Pâté Edith (page 30)

Marinade:

2   cups good-quality beer
2   teaspoons ginger
1   teaspoon peppercorns
2   bay leaves
2   tablespoons honey

1. Cut round steak in half, down the middle the long way. Then cut into 8 triangles. Reserve the trimmings to make a ninth triangle.

2. Prepare the marinade and place the pieces of beef in it. Refrigerate for 4 to 5 days, turning the beef daily. Set aside the marinade, discarding peppercorns and bay leaves. Drain beef.

3. Heat butter or margarine in large skillet over medium-high heat. Add meat and sauté, very quickly, about 1 to 2 minutes per side. Remove meat and pour out all but 2 tablespoons of fat in skillet and sauté shallots over moderate heat for about 30 seconds. Add flour and beat with a wire whisk until a thick paste forms. Gradually add the beer marinade to the paste, stirring constantly until a thick smooth sauce forms.

4. Roll out and cut disks. Place a triangle of beef in one half of the disk. Spoon a teaspoon of marinade sauce over the beef. Then place a generous teaspoon of the pâté of your choice on top of the Wellington filling before folding over and crimping. Bake as directed.

Samosa or Chicken Curry Empanada

Curries of all kinds, with their spicy flavor and spoonable texture, are just naturally good candidates for empanada making. Although beef, lamb, shellfish, and chicken all make delicious curries, chicken is our most popular.

This favorite filling is very similar to one used for a samosa, a traditional Indian pastry hors d'oeuvre.

Preparation: 30 minutes

2 tablespoons unsalted butter or margarine
1/4 cup chopped yellow onion
1 tablespoon flour
1 cup plain yogurt
2 tablespoons dry sherry
2 teaspoons curry powder
1 teaspoon brown sugar
1/2 cup diced cooked chicken
1/4 cup chopped dried apple
1/4 cup dried currants or raisins
1/4 cup peanuts
1 tablespoon candied ginger or 1 teaspoon minced fresh gingerroot

1. Heat butter and sauté onion in a saucepan or skillet until wilted, about 1 minute. Sprinkle with flour and stir to make a paste.

2. Add yogurt and sherry. Stir until smooth.

3. Add curry powder, brown sugar, chicken, apple, currants, peanuts, and ginger, stirring to combine well. Simmer until mixture is quite thick, about 10 minutes. Cool.

4. Now you are ready to roll out and fill disks.

Chicken Paprikash Empanada

In the fall of 1962 we found ourselves in Budapest negotiating with the Hungarian authorities about a documentary film we wanted to shoot. We were ensconced in a great Victorian tourist hotel where we stuffed ourselves on beer, pork goulash, and chicken paprikash. The headwaiter, Victor, was delighted with our presence, since we gave him the chance to practice his English. In exchange, he gave us this recipe.

Preparation: 20 minutes

- 2   tablespoons unsalted butter or margarine
- 1   medium yellow onion, diced
- 2   tablespoons tomato purée
- 2   tablespoons flour
- 1   cup diced cooked white chicken meat
- 1/2 cup chicken broth
- 1/2 cup dry vermouth or white wine
- 1/2 cup chopped fresh parsley
- 1   tablespoon Hungarian paprika
- 1/2 cup diced sweet peppers
       Freshly ground black pepper to taste
       Garnish: Paprika

1. Heat butter or margarine in large skillet, and sauté onion until golden but not brown.

2. Add tomato purée and stir with wire whisk until smooth.

3. Add flour and continue stirring with wire whisk until you have a thick, uniform paste.

4. Add chicken, broth, vermouth, parsley, paprika, lemon peel, sweet peppers, and pepper to taste. Simmer for about 15 minutes. Correct seasoning.

5. Now you are ready to roll out and fill disks. Sprinkle with paprika, if desired, after final egg glaze.

St. Wenceslaus Meatball Empanada

While trying to film a documentary in Prague in 1962, we met a young Czech filmmaker in St. Wenceslaus Square, the ancient center of the city. We became instant, if only temporary, friends. He took us home to his parents' apartment near the square where we talked into the night about film and politics. As we talked, our friend's mother served us delicious herbed meatballs in sour cream. In a three-way conversation (she spoke no English), we acquired the recipe, which we have enjoyed ever since. One savory meatball, placed in the center of an empanada disk, makes a most distinctive repast.

Preparation: 25 minutes

1	pound ground beef
1/2	cup finely chopped yellow onion
1	teaspoon savory
1	large egg, lightly beaten
4	tablespoons unsalted butter or margarine
2	tablespoons flour
1	cup beef stock
1	cup sour cream or plain yogurt
	Juice and grated rind of 1 large lemon
	Freshly ground pepper to taste

1. Combine beef, chopped onion, savory, and egg. Form into 8 to 10 1-inch meatballs.

2. Over very low heat, melt butter or margarine in large skillet.

3. Sauté meatballs in melted butter over moderate heat, about 2 minutes on each side. Remove meatballs with slotted spoon or spatula to platter.

4. Pouring off all but about 2 tablespoons of fat, add flour to drippings and stir with wire whisk until a thick paste forms. Slowly add stock, stirring constantly, until thick and creamy. Add sour cream or yogurt, lemon juice and rind, pepper and meatballs. Simmer, covered, about 10 minutes. Cool in sauce.

5. Now you are ready to roll out and fill disks, with 1 meatball plus sauce to cover in each disk.

Chilean Empanadas

Although we never actually crossed the border into Chile during our sojourn in Argentina, we got very close. High in the Andes near the Chilean border is the spectacular ski resort of San Carlos de Bariloche. Traditional foods don't always respect national boundaries, so while in Bariloche we feasted on numerous empanadas Chileanos. The meat ones, less sweet but reminiscent of their Argentine cousins, were always garnished with chopped eggs and olives. But the langostino *(salt-water crayfish) empanadas, in their* salsa del golfo, *were uniquely Chilean.*

Langostinos con Salsa del Golfo *(Langostinos with Sauce of the Gulf)* Filling

Preparation: 10 minutes

6 ounces fresh lobster or defrosted *langostinos* (salt-water crayfish), chopped
1/2 cup mayonnaise (preferably homemade)
1 tablespoon tomato purée
1 tablespoon cognac or brandy
1 teaspoon Dijon mustard
1/3 cup finely chopped scallions, including greens

1. Put shellfish pieces in a bowl and add remaining ingredients. Combine thoroughly.

2. Now you are ready to roll out and fill disks.

Chilean Beef

Preparation: 15 minutes

2	tablespoons olive oil
1/2	cup chopped yellow onion
1/2	pound ground beef
1	cup chopped spinach or Swiss chard
1/2	cup dry red wine
1/2	teaspoon seeded and crumbled dried chili pepper
1/4	teaspoon ground cumin
8 to 10	black olives, pitted and sliced
2	hard-boiled eggs, chopped
	Dash Tabasco
	Freshly ground black pepper to taste

1. Heat olive oil and sauté onion and beef over moderate flame, about 5 minutes.

2. Add the spinach, wine, chili pepper, cumin, black olives, eggs, and Tabasco, and cook over a moderate flame, stirring occasionally, for 10 minutes. Pepper to taste.

3. Now you are ready to roll out and fill disks.

67

Jamaican Pattie

In a small shop on Albany Avenue in Hartford, Connecticut, of all places, you can buy delicious Jamaican patties. This West Indian bakery produces a variety of breads and rolls of Caribbean origin, plus two types of patties, meat and vegetable. Both pastry turnovers are distinguished by the savor of hot cayenne pepper and their unmistakable empanada shape.

Since the meat pattie is the more typical, we give you our version here.

▲▲▲▲▲▲▲▲▲▲▲▲▲▲▲▲▲▲▲▲▲▲▲▲▲▲▲

Preparation: 25 minutes

1	pound finely ground beef
1/2	cup soft bread crumbs
1/2	cup beef broth
2	tablespoons unsalted butter or margarine
1/2	cup minced yellow onions
1	teaspoon savory
	Freshly ground black pepper or cayenne pepper to taste

1. Have your butcher grind the beef twice, or process with the steel blade of a food processor at home.

2. Combine bread crumbs with broth and let soak 1 to 2 minutes. Combine with beef.

3. Sauté beef mixture in butter or margarine over moderate flame until cooked through, about 3 minutes. Place in bowl with onions, savory, and pepper. Combine well.

4. Now you are ready to roll out and fill disks.

Jambalaya Empanada

A blending of French and African cultures created jambalaya, with the help of a goodly portion of the Mississippi Delta and a dash of Spain. This famous Creole dish has a special hearty-yet-delicate quality all its own.

If you make jambalaya and have leftovers, they will make a perfect filling for empanadas. If not, this recipe will provide you with a scaled-down version, just right for 8 to 10 entrée empanadas.

Preparation: 25 minutes

2	tablespoons raw long-grain rice
1/2	cup diced cooked ham
1/2	cup diced shrimp (frozen or partially cooked)
2	okras, sliced (canned or fresh)
1	fresh green bell pepper, chopped
1/3	cup chicken broth
2	tablespoons lemon juice
	Dash of Tabasco
1/4	cup sour cream or plain yogurt
	Freshly ground black pepper to taste

1. Combine all ingredients in a covered saucepan and bring to a boil. Immediately turn down and simmer until all liquid is absorbed. *Do not overcook!*

2. Now you are ready to roll out and fill the disks.

Mexican Empanadas

When you think of Mexican finger food, you tend to think of tacos, filled to overflowing with a variety of highly seasoned good foods. If you think about a taco, it is basically an open-ended cornmeal empanada. The taco goes back to pre-Columbian times, but whether its present shape was influenced by the empanada is anybody's guess. In any case, Mexico also boasts its share of empanadas. They are often filled with sweet fruits and served as a dessert, but sometimes they are filled with fruits and meat in what is known as a picadillo.

■■

Picadillo de Pollo *(Chicken)*

Preparation: 15 minutes

    2   tablespoons olive oil
    1   yellow onion, chopped
    2   *jalapeño* peppers, diced
  1/2   cup cubed cooked summer squash
    2   cups cubed cooked chicken
    1   banana, sliced and quartered
        Freshly ground black pepper to taste

1. Heat olive oil and sauté onion until golden.

2. Add *jalapeños,* squash, chicken, and banana. Sauté briefly until heated through. Add pepper to taste. Let cool.

3. Now you are ready to roll out and fill disks.

70

Picadillo de Carne *(Meat)*

Preparation: 15 minutes

2	tablespoons olive oil
1/4	pound ground beef
1/3	cup chopped yellow onion
1	clove garlic, minced
1/2	cup peeled, cored, and diced apple
2	*jalapeño* peppers, diced
1/4	cup raisins
1/4	cup sliced green Spanish olives
1	ripe plum tomato, peeled, seeded, and chopped fine
1/8	teaspoon thyme
	Cumin and freshly ground black pepper to taste

1. Heat olive oil and sauté beef, onion, and garlic over a moderate flame, stirring constantly for about 5 minutes.

2. Add the apple, *jalapeño* peppers, raisins, Spanish olives, tomato, and thyme, and simmer over low heat for another 10 minutes. Season with cumin and pepper to taste. Let cool.

3. Now you are ready to roll out and fill the disks.

71

Uruguayan Empanada del Queso Italiano *(Uruguayan Empanada with Italian Cheese)*

Because of its stable democratic government and its agricultural exports, Uruguay was once known as the Denmark of South America. It was a favored place of European emigration during the late nineteenth and early twentieth centuries. These European cultures are still evident and lend a peculiar melting-pot nostalgia to Montevideo, the capital city. Like Buenos Aires, its sister city across the Rio de la Plata, Montevideo has a large Italian population. This empanada/calzone, which we enjoyed at a friend's house, seems to exemplify the melting-pot theme that is so typical of Uruguay.

Preparation: 5 minutes

- 1/2 pound ricotta cheese
- 1/4 cup toasted pine nuts
- 1/4 cup minced scallions, including greens
- 1/4 teaspoon paprika
- 1/8 teaspoon nutmeg
- 2 egg yolks, lightly beaten
  Freshly ground black pepper to taste

1. Combine all ingredients in medium-size bowl.

2. Now you are ready to roll out and fill disks.

72

Moroccan Couscous Empanada

Rec keskes means "crushed small" in Arabic and is probably the origin of the word couscous. Crushed millet or wheat (semolina) is essential to the dish. The traditional couscous is a hearty savory stew with lamb, crushed grain, vegetables, and spices. We have adapted the original recipe to fit the empanada format by practicing a little rec keskes ourselves—chopping ingredients to a smaller size and limiting the liquid.

Preparation: 30 minutes

1	cup durum wheat semolina (couscous)
1	cup diced yellow onions
2	cloves garlic, minced
2	cups lamb or beef broth (preferably homemade)
1	tablespoon Worcestershire sauce
1	cup minced cooked lamb
1	cup pine nuts or almonds
1/2	cup raisins
2	small zucchini, washed and cubed
2	large tomatoes, chopped
1	teaspoon cumin
1/4	teaspoon powdered cloves
1	tablespoon cinnamon
	Pinch rosemary, crumbled
	Juice and grated rind of 2 limes

1. Cover couscous, onions, and garlic with hot broth. Let stand 30 minutes.

2. Combine all remaining ingredients with couscous and let marry for at least 30 minutes more. If filling seems a bit dry, moisten with more broth, red wine, or water.

3. Now you are ready to roll out and fill disks.

Moussaka Empanada

George and I were shooting a film near Iraklion on the island of Crete in 1962. We'd just gotten off the ship and were looking for a place to eat. A group of old men were dancing and playing music in the courtyard of a taverna fronting the harbor. Enchanted, we stopped, and were invited in. The most enticing aroma was coming from the kitchen in the rear. The cook led us into his kitchen past savory soup pots and a succulent lamb roasting over hot coals, but the dish that attracted our attention most was a kind of casserole beckoning to us with the heady aroma of cinnamon and unknown spices. It turned out to be our first moussaka. We've made moussaka and enjoyed other people's moussaka many times and many different ways since then. With all the sautéing of eggplant and draining it between paper towels, a moussaka usually takes forever to prepare. This one doesn't, and we like to think the time-saving innovations produce a moussaka quite reminiscent of that first one we enjoyed so much, so long ago.

Preparation: 30 minutes

1/2	large yellow onion, finely chopped
2	large cloves garlic, minced
1/2	cup olive oil
1	medium eggplant
1/4	pound chopped beef or lamb
1	cup dry red wine
	Juice and grated rind of 1 lemon
2	tablespoons tomato purée
1/3	cup chopped fresh parsley
2	tablespoons cinnamon
1	teaspoon oregano
	Freshly grated Parmesan to taste
	Freshly ground black pepper to taste
	Freshly grated nutmeg to taste
1 1/2	cups plain yogurt
	Garnish: Paprika

1. In large skillet, sauté onion and garlic in olive oil until golden.

2. Wash and cut the eggplant into 1/2-inch cubes, but do not peel. Add to onion and garlic, stirring constantly, about 3 minutes.

3. Add beef or lamb, stirring continuously until just cooked through, about 2 minutes. Add wine, lemon rind and juice, tomato purée, parsley, cinnamon, oregano, Parmesan, pepper, nutmeg, and yogurt. Stir well for about 1 minute.

4. Now you are ready to roll out and fill disks. Sprinkle the garnish, if desired, on top of the final egg glaze.

Chicken Parmigiana Empanada

As far as restaurants are concerned, Buenos Aires is an Italian city. During the year we lived there, we feasted in innumerable family places where the pasta was rolled and cut by hand on the back tables, and the veal parmigiana was always out of this world. Since Argentina was the home of the gaucho and the cow, and beef and veal were quite inexpensive, we often prepared veal parmigiana at home. Now, however, faced with the economic realities of life in the United States, we substitute chicken for the veal and find it equally delicious.

Preparation: 15 minutes

1 tablespoon unsalted butter or margarine
2 cloves garlic, minced
1 tablespoon minced shallots
1 cup diced cooked white chicken
1 cup tomato purée
1 teaspoon oregano
1 teaspoon dried basil
1/2 cup dry red wine
Freshly ground black pepper to taste
4 ounces mozzarella cheese, grated
Garnish: Grated Parmesan cheese, dried parsley, paprika

1. Heat butter in saucepan and sauté garlic and shallots for 1 minute. Add chicken, tomato purée, oregano, basil, wine, and pepper to taste. Simmer for about 30 minutes. Correct seasoning if necessary.

2. Remove chicken mixture from heat and stir in cheese.

3. Now you are ready to roll out and fill disks. Sprinkle with garnish, if desired, after final egg glaze.

76

Cornish Pastie

This traditional Cornish miner's lunch is a hearty, no-nonsense meat-and-potato pastry turnover. Designed for traveling across fields and down mine shafts, usually the pastie's shell is heavier than the empanada's and always carries the miner's initials cut into the crust.

The recipe below is for the popular traditional Cornish pastie. The filling is really a portable stew, and, as such, many variations are possible.

Preparation: 25 minutes

2	tablespoons unsalted butter or margarine
1	large onion, minced
1	pound round steak or mutton, cubed
2	medium turnips, diced
1/2	teaspoon freshly ground pepper
1	teaspoon coriander (optional)
1/4	teaspoon thyme
1/3	cup beef broth, milk, or water

1. Melt butter or margarine in a heavy skillet, add the onion and sauté gently until transparent.

2. Add the meat and cook until browned.

3. Add the remaining ingredients. Sauté for about 15 minutes.

4. Now you are ready to roll out and fill disks.

Sauerbraten Empanada

In the 1930s and 1940s, farming and Wisconsin went together like ham and eggs. Sherry's particular dream farm belonged to a German family whose daughter Eleanor often "helped out" her mother in the governor's residence. Every weekend Eleanor's father would collect her in his Model A Ford and take her home to the farm. Occasionally, Sherry spent the weekends on the farm with Eleanor. One of Sherry's favorite memories of these visits is the pungent aroma of sauerbraten marinating in the cool kitchen pantry. To this day, the smell of sauerbraten in its sauce of wine, vinegar, and herbs conjures up an image of that dream farm of her childhood. It also makes a heavenly empanada!

Preparation: 20 minutes

1   pound leftover pot roast, cut into
     1/2-inch slices
1/2 cup wine vinegar
1/2 cup dry red wine
1   medium yellow onion, sliced
1   teaspoon dry mustard
1   teaspoon ground ginger
1/2 teaspoon ground cloves
1   tablespoon capers
1   teaspoon peppercorns
1   bay leaf
2   cloves garlic, minced
2   tablespoons brown sugar
3   gingersnaps, crumbled
1/2 cup sour cream
     Freshly ground black pepper to taste
     Garnish: Dried parsley, paprika

1. Make a marinade of the vinegar, wine, onion, mustard, ginger, cloves, capers, peppercorns, bay leaf, garlic, and brown sugar. Pour over the slices of beef and marinate for 2 to 3 days in the refrigerator.

2. When you are ready to make your empanadas, drain the marinade from the beef and discard. Combine the drained beef with the crumbled gingersnaps, sour cream, and pepper to taste.

3. Now you are ready to roll out and fill disks. Sprinkle with garnish, if desired, after final egg glaze.

DESSERTS

In our experience, sweet dessert empanadas are much less common than the savory ones since traditionally empanadas are served as lunch or dinner. However, if you use the term *pastry turnover,* the phrase immediately conjures up a crescent- or triangular-shape individual pie, usually containing an apple, cherry, or blueberry filling. Called fried pies, they are a common commercial product in the southern United States.

You can fill an empanada shell with a single sugared fruit, but we prefer to let our imaginations wander. Combinations of ingredients often enhance one another's qualities, making for a more exciting taste. Here are some of our favorite dessert combinations, which all produce 8 to 10 6-inch empanadas. If you really want to gild the lily, a hot sweet empanada served with vanilla ice cream or yogurt is, for any occasion, true ambrosia.

Apricot and Ginger Empanada

Called Armenian plums, apricots became popular in fifteenth-century Europe and have been a favored fruit for sweet pastries ever since. It is the distinctly strong and pungent flavor of apricots that make them memorable in tarts, pastes, and preserves.

Ginger was popular a century earlier in Europe as a medicinal herb. It was much touted as a cure for the black death, the plague that was sweeping the continent at that time. But whether it can cure the plague or not, ginger has a strong aromatic flavor that adds a lively zest to a wide variety of foods.

Two strong characters don't always make a happy marriage, but in this recipe these two strong flavors blend beautifully to make a delicious sweet and spicy dessert empanada.

Preparation: 5 minutes

1	cup chopped dried apricots
1/2	cup apricot jam
1/2	teaspoon ground ginger

Garnish: Confectioner's sugar

1. Combine apricots with jam and ginger.

2. Now you are ready to roll out and fill disks.

3. After baking, dust with confectioner's sugar.

Bananas de Estancia

It was at an old estancia (ranch) southeast of Buenos Aires where we first tasted this combinaton of ingredients. We had been out scouting locations for a film with the owners. It was late by the time we got back. With profuse apologies for not having time for a proper asado (a variety of grilled meats), the wife served us a delicious meal. Then she disappeared into the kitchen and came back moments later with a simple yet distinctive dessert. We have enjoyed it many times since then, both in and out of empanada shells. But with the shell it is a more complete and satisfying finale to a delicious meal.

Preparation: 10 minutes

2	ripe bananas, sliced
2	tablespoons lemon juice
1	teaspoon cinnamon
2	tablespoons brown sugar
1/4	cup rum
1 1/2	cup sour cream or yogurt

Garnish: Confectioner's sugar, cinnamon

1. Place bananas, lemon juice, cinnamon, brown sugar, rum, and sour cream in a bowl and toss like a salad to distribute evenly. Let rest for 15 to 20 minutes.

2. Now you are ready to roll out and fill disks.

3. Dust with confectioner's sugar and/or cinnamon after baking.

Cherry and Walnut Empanada

This is one of those empanadas that just happened. Friends dropped in unexpectedly. Luckily, we had enough for dinner, but not a thing for dessert. A quick scan of the pantry revealed a jar of Bing cherries, walnuts, and some grated coconut. There were some empanada disks and sour cream in the refrigerator. And in that moment, this impromptu empanada was born.

We've made other empanadas at a moment's notice, and you can too. Simply take a look at what's at hand, then let your imagination be your guide. Some turn out better than others, but we've never had a real disaster.

▲▲▲▲▲▲▲▲▲▲▲▲▲▲▲▲▲▲▲▲▲▲▲▲▲

Preparation: 20 minutes

1 8¹/₂-ounce can pitted Bing cherries, drained
¹/₃ cup chopped walnuts
¹/₃ cup grated coconut
¹/₃ cup sour cream
¹/₄ cup granulated sugar
Garnish: Confectioner's sugar

1. Combine drained cherries with walnuts, coconut, sour cream, and granulated sugar.

2. Now you are ready to roll out and fill disks.

3. After baking, dust with confectioner's sugar.

Peach Melba Empanadas

We don't know who the genius was who first thought of combining the flavors of peaches and raspberries. Maybe it was accidental. But these two flavors naturally have a great affinity. In this recipe their magic is worked with the utmost simplicity and the least effort.

Preparation: 5 minutes

1/2 cup good-quality raspberry jam
1 8 1/2-ounce can Elberta peach slices, drained and cut in half
Cinnamon and ground ginger to taste
Garnish: Confectioner's sugar

1. Roll out dough and cut disks.

2. Place 1 scant tablespoon of jam in center of each disk. Now add 2 to 4 small peach halves, sprinkle with cinnamon and ginger, fold over, and crimp the pastry with a fork.

Mixed Fruit Turnovers

Apple turnovers are good and lots of people make them, but we think spiced apples and apricot turnovers are even better! Blueberry pie is good, too, but we think this berry is even tastier combined with bananas, cinnamon, and lemon. This mixing of fruits in pies, tarts, and turnovers got started in our family a long time ago. Here are three of our favorites.

Strawberry-Rhubarb Filling

Preparation: 30 minutes

1	tablespoon cornstarch
1/2	cup lemon juice
1	tablespoon grated lemon rind
1	cup chopped fresh rhubarb
1	cup ripe strawberries
2	tablespoons freshly chopped ginger
2	tablespoons flour
3/4	cup sugar
	Garnish: Confectioner's sugar

1. Combine cornstarch with lemon juice and rind.

2. Steam rhubarb in top of double boiler for about 10 minutes.

3. Wash and hull strawberries, and cut in half.

4. Combine all ingredients except confectioner's sugar. Let stand for 15 to 20 minutes.

5. Now you are ready to roll out and fill disks.

6. After baking, dust with confectioner's sugar.

Blueberry and Banana Filling

Preparation: 10 minutes

1	tablespoon cornstarch
1/4	cup lemon juice
	Grated rind of 1/2 lemon
1	cup fresh blueberries
1	cup chopped bananas
1	teaspoon cinnamon
1/8	teaspoon nutmeg
1/2	cup sugar

Garnish: Confectioner's sugar

1. Combine all ingredients except confectioner's sugar. Let stand 15 to 20 minutes.

2. Now you are ready to roll out and fill disks.

3. After baking, dust with confectioner's sugar.

Apple and Apricot Filling

Preparation: 10 minutes

1	cup chopped dried apples
1/2	cup apricot jam
1/4	cup lemon juice
	Grated rind of 1/2 lemon
1/4	teaspoon coriander

Garnish: Confectioner's sugar

1. Combine all ingredients except confectioner's sugar.

2. Now you are ready to roll out and fill disks.

3. After baking, dust with confectioner's sugar.

Nancy's Cream Cheese and Chutney Empanada

Our friend Nancy, who brought Sweet Potatoes Supreme (page 48) into our life, also was the first to serve us this peculiar-sounding but delicious combination. It makes a creamy, sweet, and spicy spread, which she served on crackers as an hors d'oeuvre. We experimented with this savory mix inside an empanada shell and decided we preferred it as a dessert. It is also good all by itself as a snack. You can use prepared chutney, but we prefer Nancy's.

Preparation: 15 minutes

12	ounces cream cheese
1¹/₂	cups commercial chutney or Nancy's Chutney

Nancy's Chutney

2	cups cider vinegar
2	cups canned apricots, drained
1	cup raisins
1	fresh pineapple, chopped, or 2 cups canned
1	cup firm, fresh peaches, peeled, pitted, and diced (or, if unavailable, canned peaches)
2	peeled mangoes, chopped (optional)
1	medium yellow onion, diced
	Juice and rind of 3 limes
2¹/₂	cups packed brown sugar

Have ready in a clean cloth bag, tied:

2	sticks cinnamon
2	tablespoons mustard seeds
2	tablespoons whole cloves
2	teaspoons ground ginger

1. To make Nancy's chutney, place all ingredients (except cream cheese) in stainless steel or enameled Dutch oven. Bring to boil, simmer uncovered, stirring occasionally until chutney thickens, 1 to 1¹/₂ hours. Remove bag of spices. Cool and store in refrigerator. Chutney can be kept 2 to 3 weeks.

2. Combine chutney with cream cheese.

3. Now you are ready to roll out and fill disks.

Ricotta Surprise

We call this ricotta surprise because this smooth Italian cheese just doesn't sound like dessert. However, mixed with fresh fruit, chocolate chips, rum, and spices, ricotta makes a surprisingly light and delicious dessert empanada.

Preparation: 15 minutes

- 1/2 pound ricotta cheese
- 1/4 cup granulated sugar
- 1/4 cup dark rum
- 1/2 teaspoon ground cinnamon
- 1 teaspoon grated lemon rind
- 1/2 cup fraise du bois (tiny whole strawberries) or fresh blueberries
- 1/2 cup chocolate chips
- 2 eggs, beaten
  Garnish: Confectioner's sugar, ground cinnamon

1. Combine ricotta with sugar, rum, and cinnamon. Whip with fork until creamy.

2. Fold in lemon rind, fraise du bois or blueberries, and chocolate chips. All ingredients should be evenly distributed.

3. Now you are ready to roll out and fill disks.

4. Glaze with egg and garnish with confectioner's sugar and cinnamon.

Note: It is essential in this recipe that fruit be fresh and unfrozen.

Walnut and Coconut Crunch Empanada

This is another dessert empanada we just put together one evening when we were looking for that "something different" to serve. It is granola's elegant cousin, and although created for dessert, it is also a favorite for late-night eating and is a good snack for the day hiker.

Preparation: 20 minutes

- 1/2   cup brown sugar
- 1/2   cup chopped walnuts
- 1/2   cup flaked coconut
- 1   large egg, beaten
- 1   teaspoon rum
- 1   tablespoon flour

Garnish: Confectioner's sugar

1. Combine all ingredients except confectioner's sugar.

2. Now you are ready to roll out and fill disks.

3. After baking, dust with confectioner's sugar.

Rumtopf Renouf Empanada

Rumtopf got started in our family with an old crock that Sherry had picked up in a secondhand store. The crock was decorated with fruits, a paragraph in German, and the single word RUMTOPF *in bold letters. We asked an Alsatian artist friend, Edward Renouf, about rumtopf. He translated the German that told us how a proper rumtopf is made: Fresh fruits are layered in the crock along with specific amounts of rum and sugar. What takes place over a period of months is something we all learned about in grade-school biology: osmosis. The rum and sugar preserve the fruits and make them juicier and sweeter than they were when first placed in the crock.*

To make rumtopf, you will need a 2-quart stoneware crock (don't use metal or glass) with a close-fitting top. Most fruits can be used, although you should avoid mushy fruits (such as bananas) in general, and blackberries, strawberries, and raspberries in particular. Over the years we've found that seedless green grapes, mangoes, seeded Bing cherries, pineapple, and sliced plums and peaches marry well. Mixed with yogurt, rumtopf makes a superb dessert empanada filling.

Preparation: 20 minutes

1   quart light or dark rum
2   sticks cinnamon
1   cup of sugar for every cup of fresh
    fruit
1   cup (approximately) yogurt to 3 cups
    fruit

1. To make rumtopf, pour rum into crock, along with cinnamon sticks.

2. Pour 1 cup of fresh fruit (we usually start with blueberries) and 1 cup of sugar into crock. Stir briefly morning and night, for 2 or 3 days, until sugar is dissolved. Then you are ready to add the next cup of sugar and cup of fruit as it comes into season. Only you will know when your rumtopf is ready and you are ready for your rumtopf, but you should leave the crock unopened for at least 3 to 4 weeks after adding the final cup of fruit and sugar.

3. To use as a filling, mix 3 cups *drained* rumtopf to approximately 1 cup yogurt.

4. Now you are ready to roll out and fill disks.

Index

About the Authors   Educational and feature filmmakers for eighteen years, Sherry and George Zabriskie turned to food making after Sherry was given the 1980 Tiffany Silver Spoon Award for her Argentine Spiced Beef Empanada by *Woman's Day*. Since then, they have sold more than one hundred thousand of their homemade empanadas in retail markets throughout New York and Connecticut. The Zabriskies have also written food articles for Pan Am's *Clipper* magazine, the *New York Post*, and *Working Woman*. Recently, they opened a gourmet takeout store and catering firm, Savories, in Sharon, Connecticut.